DISCOVER SERIES
GEMAS

Arete Ámbar Y Anillo

Ágata Blanco y Negro

Ágate Azul

Ágate Verde Azul

Zafiro Azul

Chacancanita

Citrina

Cambio de Color Granate

Piedras Preciosas de Colores

Diamante

Esmeralda

Fluorita

Collar de Cuentas Verdes

Ónix

Piedras Rosas y Azules

Zafiro Rosa

Piedras Preciosas

Cuarzo Púrpura

Scapolite

Cuarzo Púrpura

Granate de Rodiolita

Turmalina Rubellita

Rubí

Aretes Serpentina

Obsidiana Copo de Nieve

Make Sure to Check Out the Other Discover Series Books from Xist Publishing:

Published in the United States by Xist Publishing
www.xistpublishing.com
PO Box 61593 Irvine, CA 92602

© 2018 by Xist Publishing All rights reserved
Translated by Victor Santana
No portion of this book may be reproduced without express permission of the publisher
All images licensed from Fotolia
First Spanish Edition

ISBN: 978-1-5324-0713-0   eISBN: 978-1-5324-0714-7

xist Publishing

www.ingramcontent.com/pod-product-compliance
Lightning Source LLC
LaVergne TN
LVHW070950070426
835507LV00030B/3478